From Se
to Sandwich

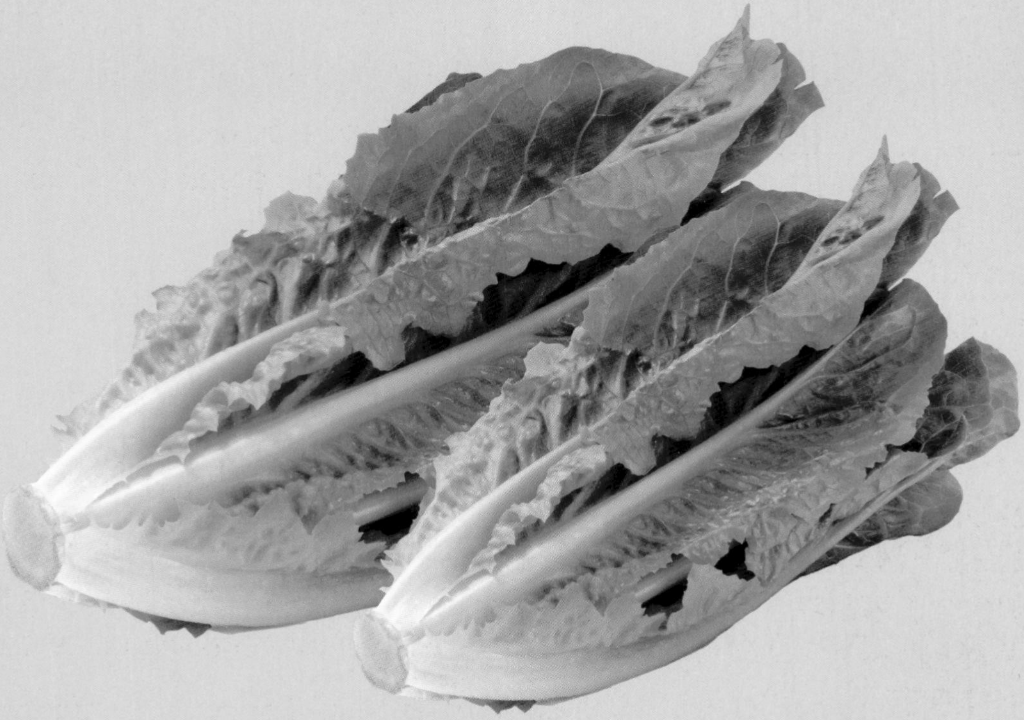

Written by Fiona Kent

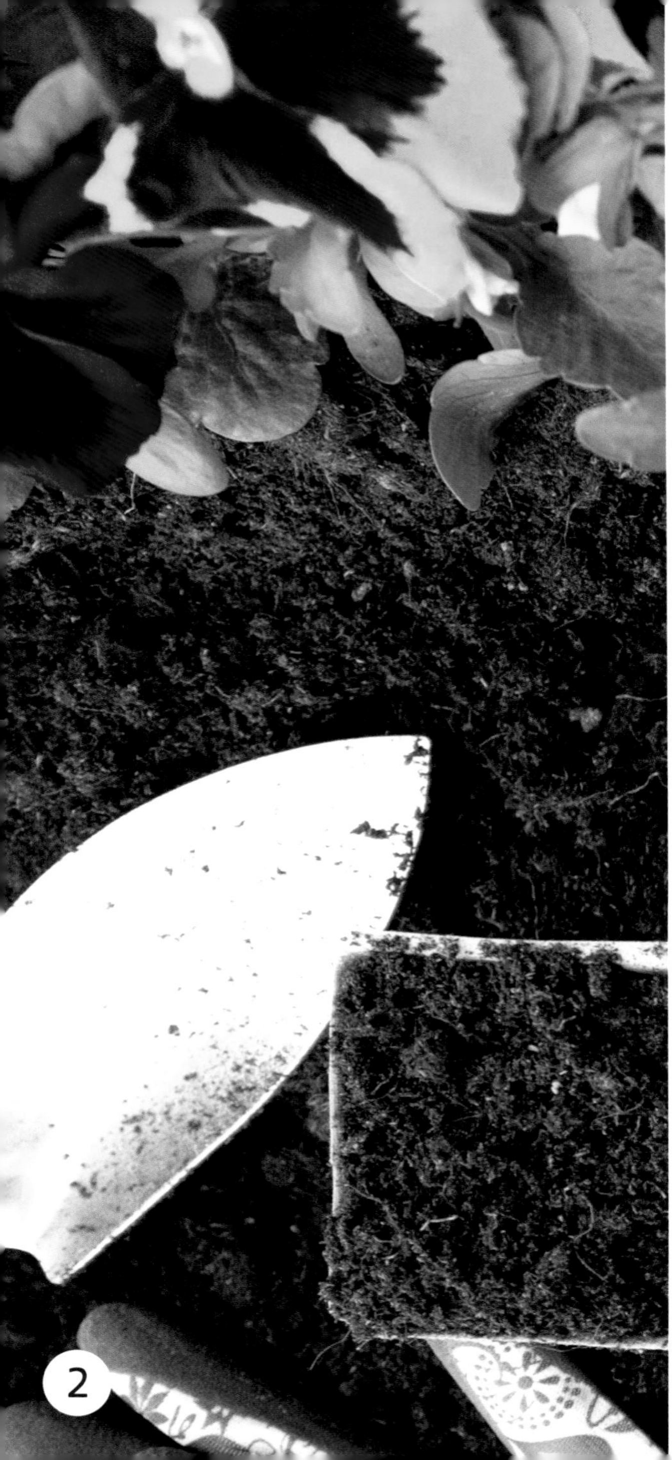
2

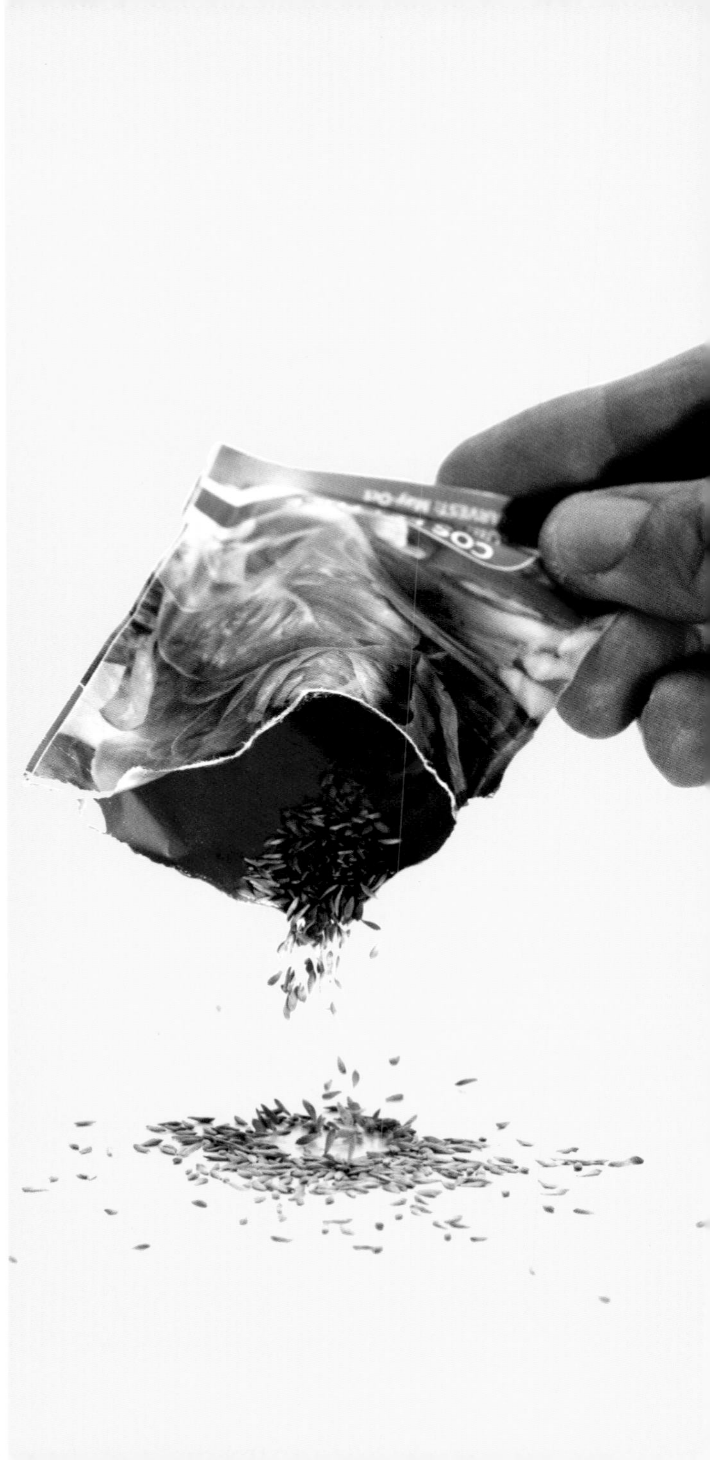

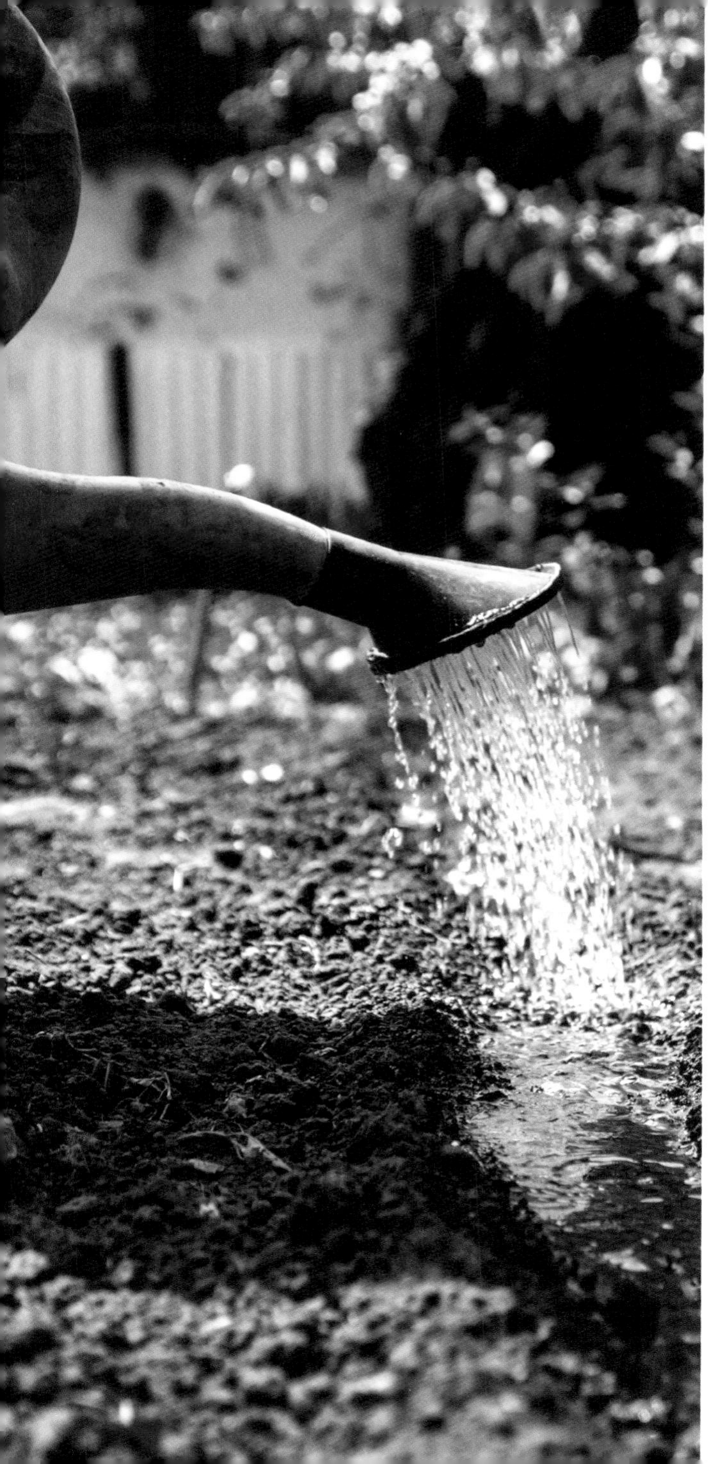
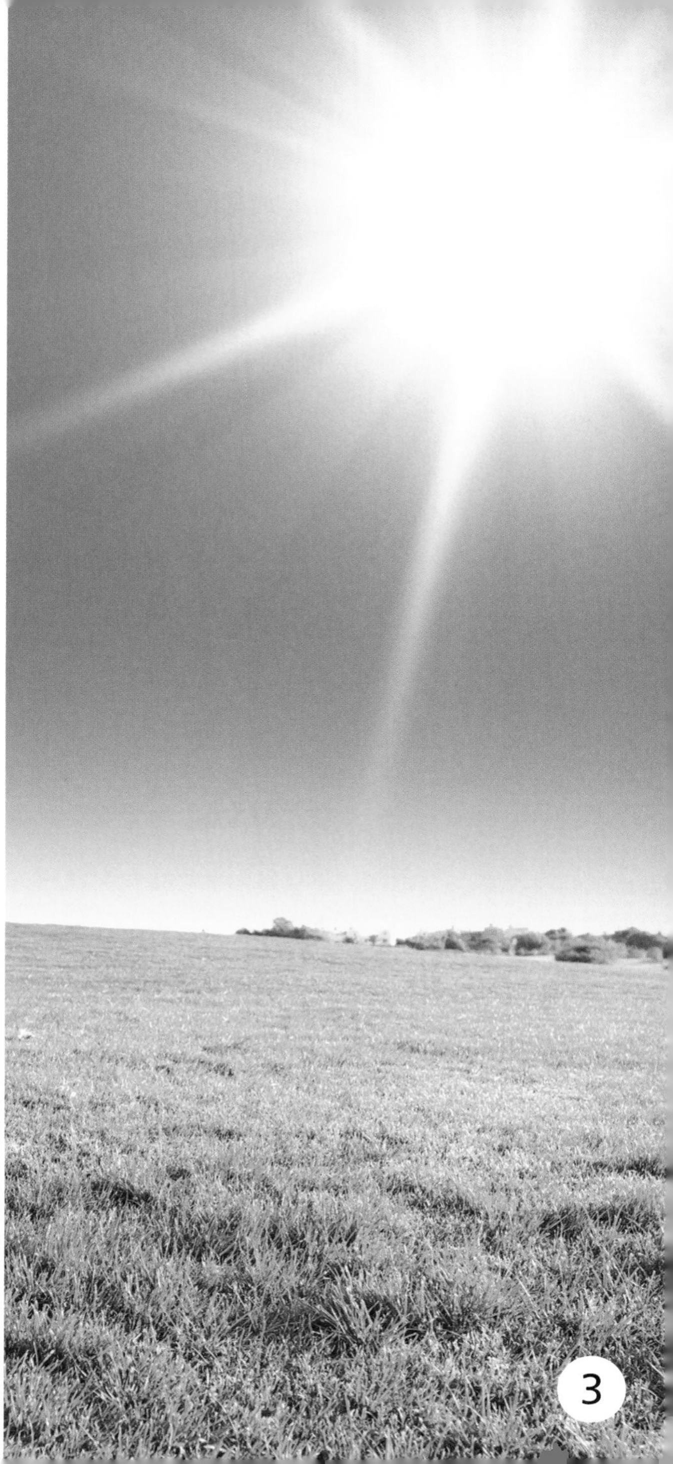

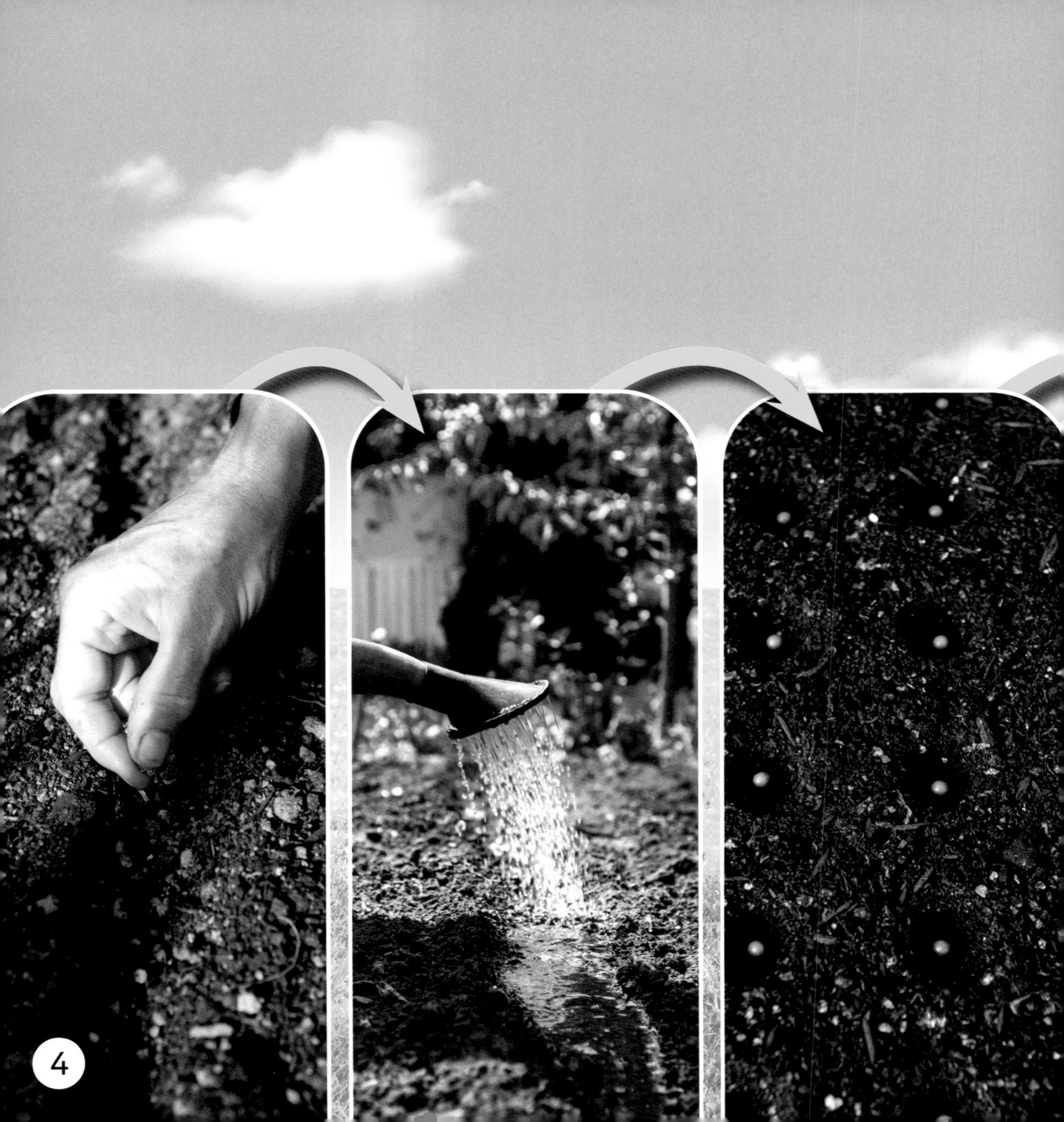

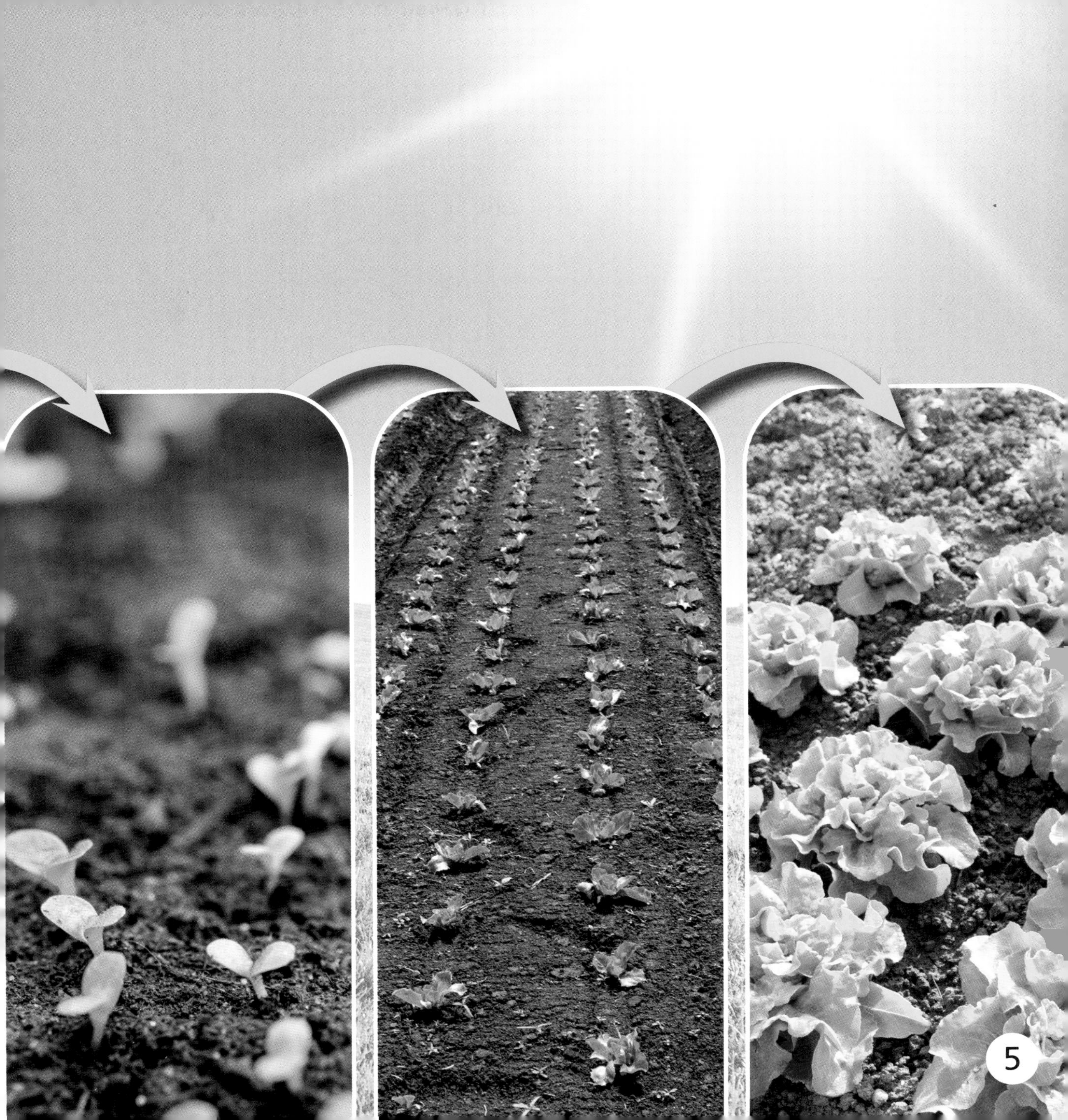

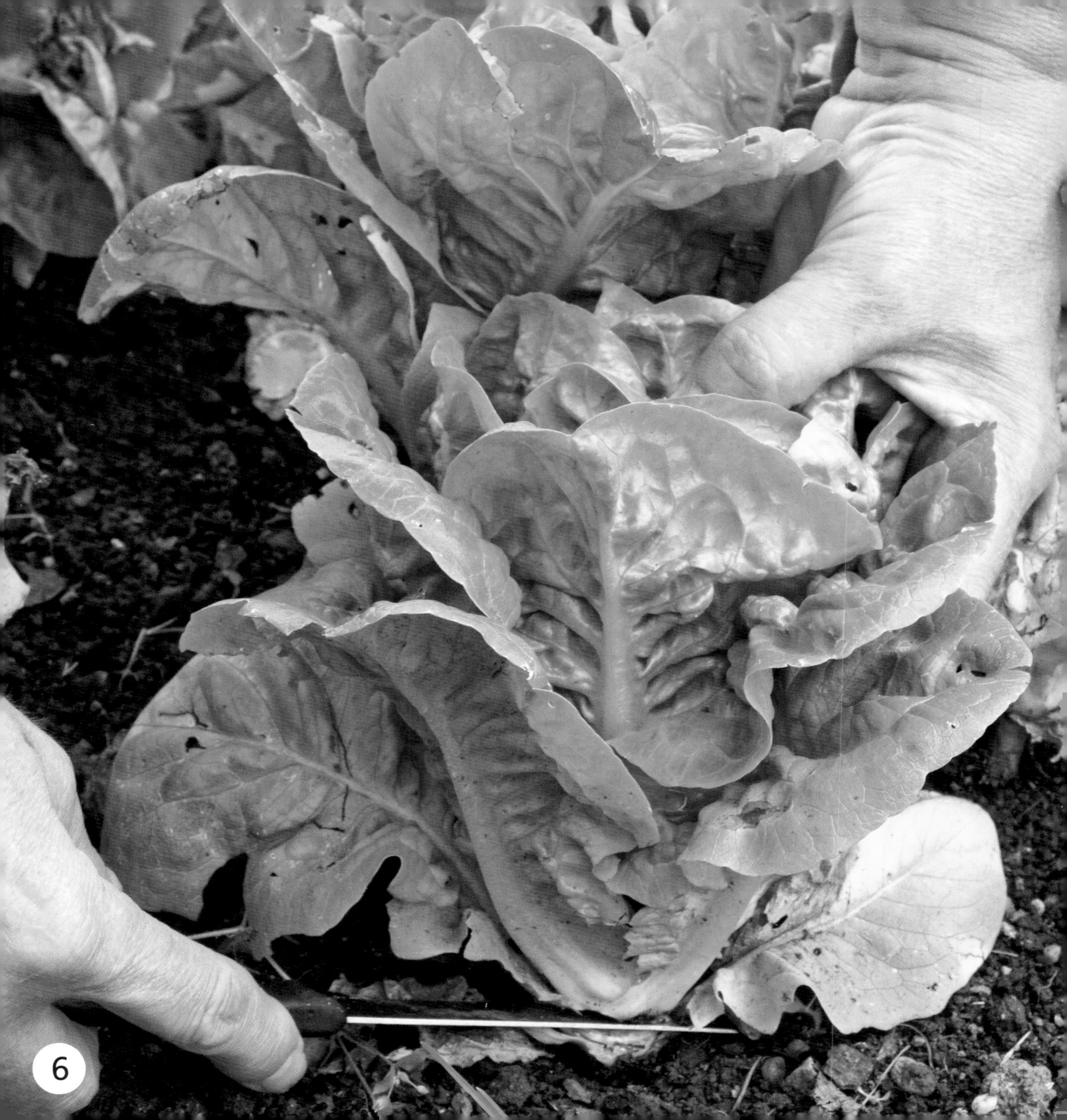
6

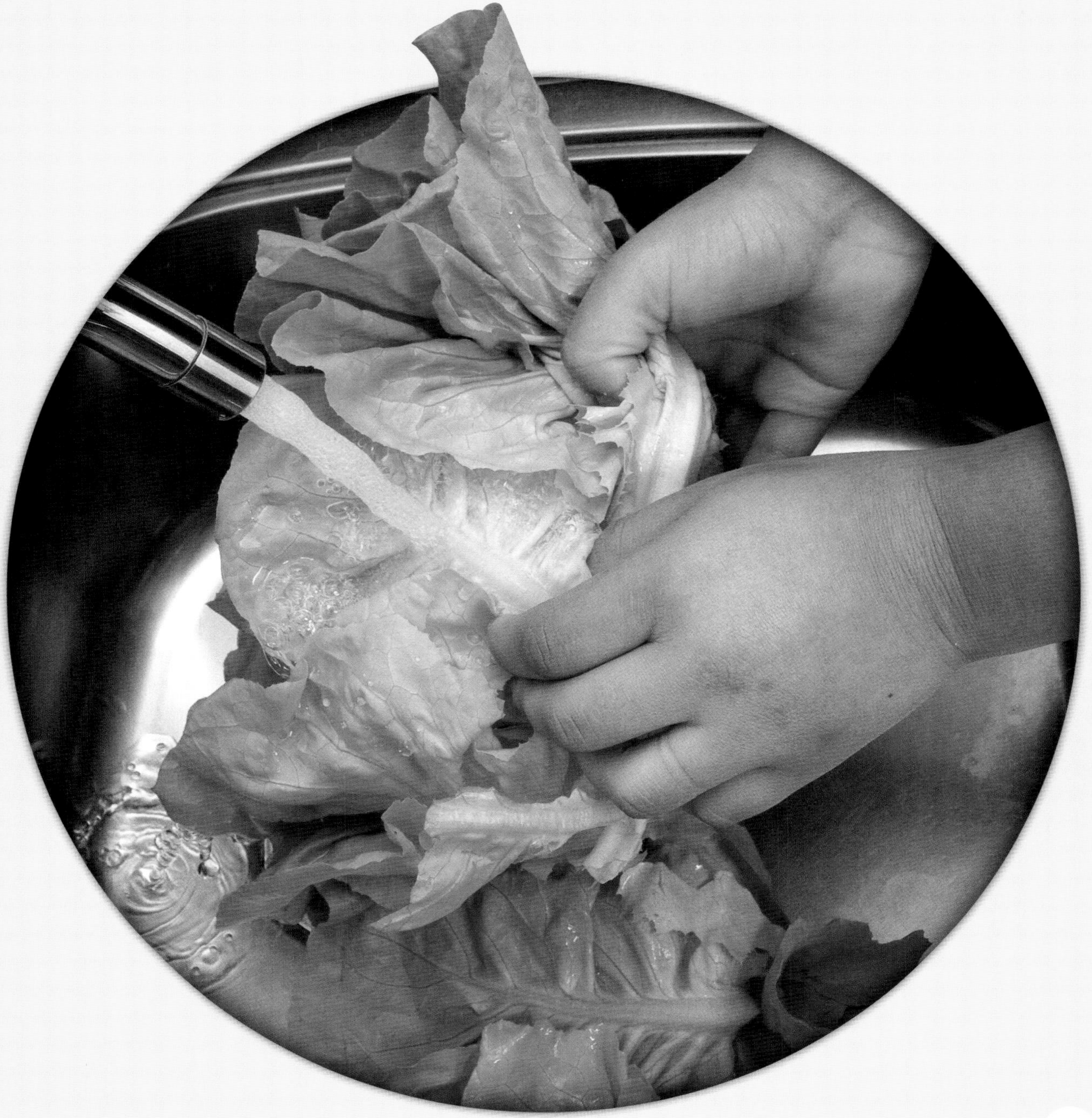

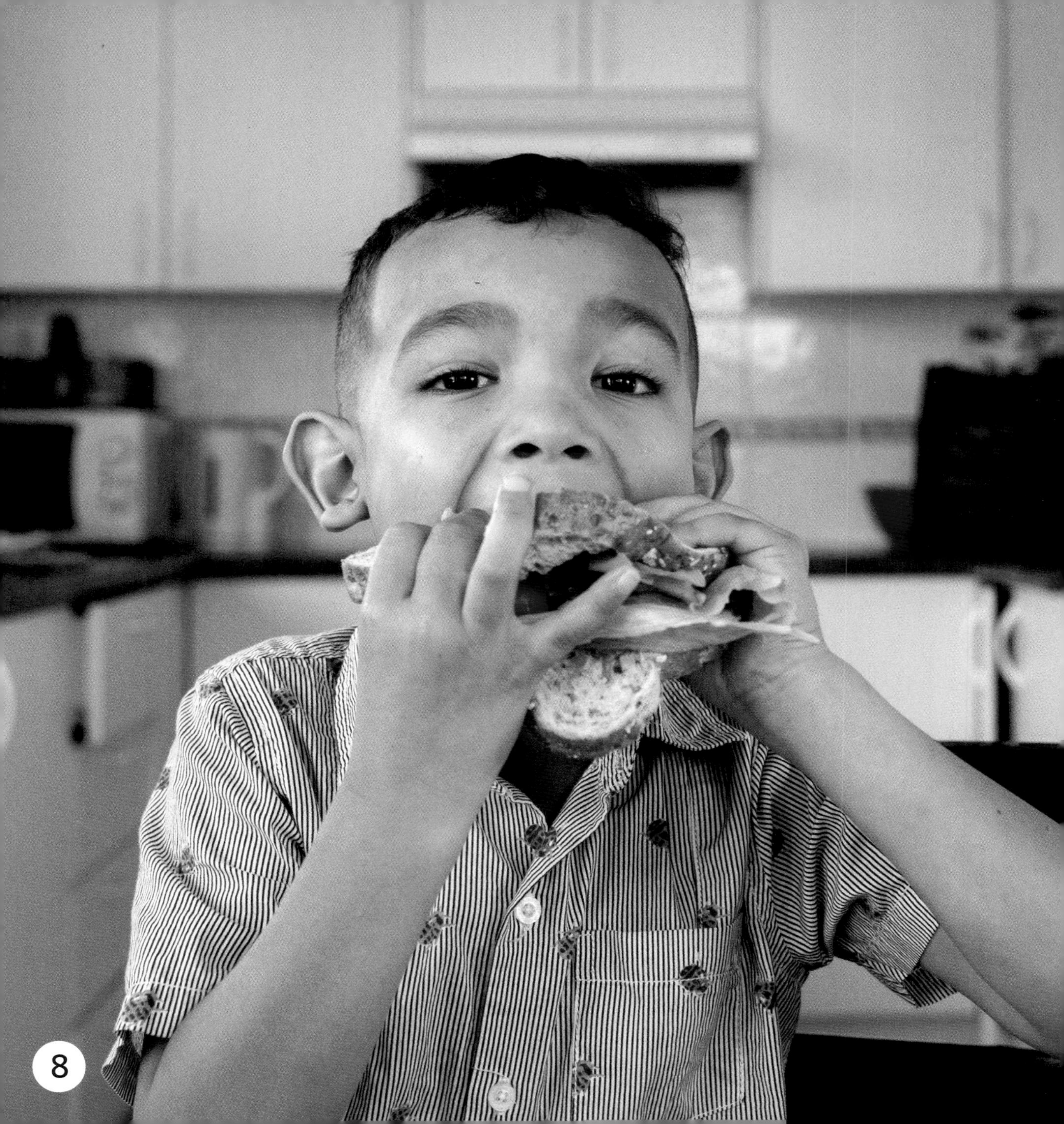